The

NO EXCUSE
Travel Planner

An Interactive Travel Planner

for Taking Immediate Action

by Philipp Gloeckl

Publisher: Philipp Gloeckl

ISBN: 978-1-7356453-4-6

If you happen to find this travel planner on a park bench somewhere, please return it to: _____

The NO EXCUSE Travel Planner is not your usual travel planner. It's packed with useful tips, helpful goals and all the exciting steps needed to make planning your perfect trip effortless and exciting. So, take a moment to congratulate yourself. You're one step closer to fulfilling your travel goals with this interactive travel planner, designed to help you make exponential use of your time to create the perfect travel experience. Set out on life's greatest adventure in 12 months or less!

HOW TO WORK WITH THIS PLANNER

Unlike other planners, the NO EXCUSE Travel Planner starts with the end goal in mind, then walks you through all the most important steps needed to prepare for your trip, with clear action plans and measurable goals to make sure you're ready.

This travel planner aids in mastering practical challenges, leading you to an inspired place where you'll have all the tools you need for a happy and fulfilling life of travel.

Take the time to develop a good travel planning habit by writing down your progress and ticking off the must-dos to avoid making excuses. Each month will bring you closer to your departure date, giving you at most a year to make your arrangements. You may you find you plough through your planning much faster than anticipated - that's absolutely okay! If you're ready to travel sooner, travel sooner! If you need to take your time getting organized, don't take more than a year to get your plans in place.

The world is yours, reach out and take it!
TravelPeeGee

I'M TAKING THIS TRIP BECAUSE I HOPE TO:

12 MONTHS TO GO...

MONTH 1
START WITH A TRAVEL VISION

'The biggest adventure you can take is to live the life of your dreams.'

- OPRAH WINFREY

Creating the perfect travel vision is all about dreaming, so put aside your worries and really delve deep into all the things that inspire you to travel!

This is the month to explore your own city, to discover the things you love and to practice feeling comfortable spending time alone. Visit libraries, scroll through the shelves in quaint second-hand bookshops, sip coffee in the local squares and try out some new restaurants you may not have dared to visit previously.

Develop your mood for travel, stretch yourself and see where your imagination can take you. Write it all down with dedication and commitment, never allowing yourself to fall into the easiest option just because it's what you know. Push your thoughts and let them run free...

GET YOUR FUTURE FINANCES IN ORDER

Firstly, open a new bank account and create a dedicated travel hub for your finances. Keep a notebook to track your travel savings, and make sure your travel account is kept separate from your normal spending. This will help you to stop thinking about how you'll afford your travel plans, and let you think about the experiences you'll want to have while you're off on your adventure!

CREATE AN INSPIRATION BOARD

Your mood board can be anything from a dedicated Pinterest board filled with travel ideas, to a box of magazine clippings and inspirational quotes. Gather your ideas in one place so you can look at it all at once and see where you feel naturally drawn to. You won't love everything about every country, so try to follow your natural sense of curiosity to see where it takes you.

LOOK AT WEBSITES THAT SELL GROUP TOURS

Whether you're planning to travel with others or set out on your own, group tour websites are a brilliant resource for planning the perfect trip. Adventure tours visit the most popular places, stay for just the right amount of time and usually throw in a few surprises for added variety. These make great templates for the perfect itineraries, and always work well logistically, so don't be afraid to follow similar routes even if you decide to travel independently.

DEVELOP YOUR EYE FOR ADVENTURE

Think about some of the amazing things you can discover in your hometown. View your city or village with tourist eyes, looking for all the things that inspire you in your everyday activities. Read books, and look for new special places every day.

10 Travel Books to Read	10 Attractions to Visit	10 Hidden Gems Found
The NO EXCUSE Travel Guide		

What can you experience in your hometown without spending a cent?

MONTH 1: TRACK YOUR WEEKLY PROGRESS

WEEK 1

WEEK 2

WEEK 3

WEEK 4

'Live life with no excuses, travel with no regret.'

- OSCAR WILDE

NOTES:

'Whether you think you can, or you think you can't - you're right.'

- Henry Ford

COMBAT YOUR EXCUSES WITH AN ACTION PLAN

This month my biggest excuse, worry or fear about travel has been:

I can combat this excuse with the following actions:

MONTH 1 CHECKLIST:

- ☐ OPENED A DEDICATED TRAVEL FUND SAVINGS ACCOUNT
- ☐ CREATED MY TRAVEL INSPIRATION BOARD
- ☐ RESEARCHED SMALL GROUP TOURS & ITINERARIES
- ☐ EXPLORED MY OWN HOMETOWN AS A TOURIST
- ☐ DISCOVERED NEW EXPERIENCES OUTSIDE MY COMFORT ZONE
- ☐ MADE A LIST OF GREAT TRAVEL BOOKS TO READ

MONTH 2
MAKE YOUR TRAVEL VISION SUSTAINABLE

Now that you have your ideas flowing freely, take some time to think about how you can support your travels while you're away. For some people, this means setting up a small business that can be managed remotely. For others, getting part-time work along the way brings in the income needed for the next part of the journey.

Think about your skills and experience, as well as what kinds of work you may like to do. It's also helpful to define your red line around the things you're not interested in, which will make finding a stream of income even easier.

My Top Skills	Work I Find Fulfilling	Work I Don't Enjoy Doing

THINK OUTSIDE THE BOX

Finding a travel-friendly job is different from finding a normal job. For traveler jobs, the main objectives should be to earn enough money to allow for more travels, to open opportunities to meet interesting people, to discover new cultures, and to learn valuable soft skills that can help you progress your career in later life.

There's a balancing act in getting the right kinds of work to sustain a lifetime of travel. Having mobile work that can happen anywhere lets you travel for extended periods of time without needing to worry much about getting back to work. Having a distinguished career in your hometown lets you travel often, for shorter periods.

How you balance this within your own life is always a personal choice. As a traveler, try to think laterally about the kinds of work you may be able to do if you wish to travel for a few months or years. Some great starting points for traveler work include:

- ✈ Launching an online drop shipping business or running an Etsy store
- ✈ Working in hotels, lodges or resorts in popular tourist location
- ✈ Fruit picking or doing seasonal farm work
- ✈ Traveling the world as crew on a cruise ship
- ✈ Freelancing as a copywriter, social media manager or content developer
- ✈ Running a blog with affiliate links as a digital nomad
- ✈ Volunteering abroad
- ✈ Virtual assistant, temporary office work or local part time employment

TOP TIP!

Tourism is a great industry for long-term travelers to find work, especially in places that offer live-in work with free living expenses.

If you follow the seasons, for example working the winter in a ski resort in Queenstown, New Zealand, then moving to the Bay of Islands to work the summer, you'll be able to save up most of your earnings, while experiencing two very different sides to New Zealand as a local.

Whenever you find something good, add it to your mood board or keep a clipping in your online bookmarks to refer to later. This will help you refine your ideas and come up with a plan to earn money while you're having fun.

MONTH 2 CHECKLIST:

- ☐ PULLED OUT MY OLD RESUMES TO CONSOLIDATE MY SKILLS
- ☐ RESEARCHED SEASONALITY IN THE COUNTRIES I WISH TO VISIT
- ☐ MADE A LIST OF THINGS I'M WILLING TO DO TO EARN MONEY
- ☐ LOOKED AT TRAVEL BLOGS
- ☐ VISITED BACKPACKER BOARDS & FREELANCING WEBSITES
- ☐ EXPLORED ONLINE STORES SUCH AS SHOPIFY & ETSY

MONTH 2: TRACK YOUR WEEKLY PROGRESS

WEEK 1

WEEK 2

WEEK 3

WEEK 4

'Live life with no excuses, travel with no regret.'

- OSCAR WILDE

NOTES:

'Whether you think you can, or you think you can't - you're right.'

- Henry Ford

MONTH 3
COMMIT TO BECOMING A TRAVELER

'It doesn't matter where you are. You are nowhere compared to where you can go.'

- BOB PROCTOR

This is one of the most important and exciting times in the travel planning process. It's the month you pick a departure date and book your flight! Once this is done, all your excuses will melt away and your travel plans will become real!

VISIT A TRAVEL AGENT

You may be thinking the best way to book a flight is to go online and find the cheapest seat on the cheapest flight. This can be a tempting way to do it, but the best way to get the most value for your money is to work with a travel agent. Travel agents have access to Round-the-World tickets, allowing you to connect multiple countries and destinations on the same ticket, with little extra cost.

If done right, a Round-the-World ticket with the right stops, in the right order, can cost about the same as a single one-way international ticket to just one destination.

Once you have a list of the places you wish to travel to, and the amount of time you have available, give it to a trusted travel agent to work their magic for the cheapest flights using the most efficient routing - saving you time and money!

TIPS FOR FINDING THE CHEAPEST INTERNATIONAL FLIGHTS

✈ Not all the seats on the same flight cost the same. Flights get more expensive the closer you get to your departure date. Fares also rise as the plane fills up, so the sweet spot is to book your flights 11 months before departure, as soon as they're released for sale.

✈ The cheapest day of the week to fly is Tuesday. Be flexible. Sometimes a slight change to your date or plan can cut the cost of your flights in half.

✈ Try to avoid flying during school vacations or over major holidays.

✈ Most airlines allow a complimentary stopover in their home city, such as Dubai or Hong Kong. If you're flying a long way, it's worth including a free stay between flights to add an extra destination without an extra flight.

✈ Many airlines work together to operate shared routes. This means you can often fly to a destination not offered by an airline, without buying an extra ticket. These types of flights offer some outstanding value on challenging routes, such as visiting Bali on the way to Australia.

✈ South America, Australia & New Zealand, as well as much of South East Asia, offer regional flight add-ons and discounted domestic flights that are booked alongside your international flight. These can be very cheap!

MONTH 3: TRACK YOUR WEEKLY PROGRESS

WEEK 1

WEEK 2

WEEK 3

WEEK 4

'Live life with no excuses, travel with no regret.'

- OSCAR WILDE

NOTES:

'Whether you think you can, or you think you can't - you're right.'

- Henry Ford

DISARM YOUR EXCUSES BY MAKING A PLAN

This month my biggest excuse, worry or fear about booking flights has been:

I can combat this excuse/worry/fear with the following actions:

MONTH 3 CHECKLIST:

- ☐ DECIDE ON AN IDEAL DEPARTURE DATE RANGE
- ☐ MAKE A LIST OF PLACES TO VISIT ON THE ITINERARY
- ☐ PLAN THE APPROXIMATE AMOUNT OF TIME NEEDED IN EACH PLACE
- ☐ VISIT A TRAVEL AGENT TO EXPLORE THE CHEAPEST WAYS TO FLY
- ☐ ASK ABOUT OPTIONS TO BOOK WITH JUST A DEPOSIT TO PAY LATER
- ☐ BOOK AND CONFIRM FLIGHTS, WITH A CLEAR FLY DATE

MY DREAM TRAVEL ADVENTURE HAS BEEN BOOKED!

Departure Date: _____

Airline: _____

Destination: _____

MONTH 4
GET YOUR PAPERWORK IN ORDER

Congratulations! With your flights booked, your plan is now as real and as tangible as every day leading up to your travels. This is one of the most exciting parts of the planning process, so head out and tell as many people as possible about your upcoming adventure!

This is also the month for admin, so once you have your flight route in place it's time to really scrutinize your itinerary to make sure you have all the right paperwork in place for your trip.

APPLY FOR, OR RENEW, YOUR PASSPORT

Check your passport is valid for at least 6 months longer than you intend to be away for. If your passport has less than 2 to 3 years validity left on it, apply for a new one. Once you've left your home country it takes much longer to renew a passport, so you want to make sure you leave as many doors open as possible in case you decide to travel for longer than you thought you would.

If your passport is nearly full (lucky you!), but still has a few years left before it expires, you may be able to apply for extra pages to be added to your existing passport. Some countries, like South Africa, also require you to have two blank pages next to each other for border control to stamp the pages on arrival.

APPLY FOR VISAS

Applying for visas will vary depending on which countries you plan to visit. Some destinations offer a 10-year visa, while others provide shorter visas that need to be applied for closer to your departure date. You might also need a special work visa.

It's best to be organized when it comes to visas. Depending on where you are traveling to, you may be able to get your visas on arrival, but oftentimes applying for a visa needs to be done in person at the relevant embassy. You should make an appointment to do this, which can have delays of a few weeks or even months.

Write a complete list of all the visa requirements for the countries you hope to visit, then keep a note of any important dates in your diary to make sure you apply for your visas in good time. Expect delays, and plan accordingly!

GET AN INTERNATIONAL DRIVERS LICENSE

Road trips and converted campervans are popular with travelers. Most countries will allow you to drive or rent a car, provided your license is in English, but some countries have restrictions depending on which side of the road you usually drive on at home. Apply for an international driver's license that lets you drive in any country, on any side of the road. This will serve you well when you wish to deviate from the beaten track on your travels.

WRITE DOWN YOUR COUNTRIES

Take some time to pick your planned itinerary apart and write down all the countries you will be visiting. Don't forget those places you will transit through!

Countries to Visit	Visa Application Date	Visa Obtained

MONTH 4 CHECKLIST:

- ☐ RECORD IMPORTANT DATES FOR VISA APPLICATIONS
- ☐ APPLY FOR A NEW PASSPORT, OR RENEW EXISTING PASSPORT
- ☐ GET AN INTERNATIONAL DRIVER'S LICENSE
- ☐ MAKE CERTIFIED COPIES OF IMPORTANT PERSONAL DOCUMENTS

MONTH 4: TRACK YOUR WEEKLY PROGRESS

WEEK 1

WEEK 2

WEEK 3

WEEK 4

'Live life with no excuses, travel with no regret.'

- Oscar Wilde

NOTES:

'Whether you think you can, or you think you can't - you're right.'

- Henry Ford

TOP TIP!

Make sure you always have access to your most important documents in a paper format, just in case you run into any unexpected challenges abroad.

Pack a few extra passport photos, as well as certified copies of your passport, international driver's license, photo ID and birth certificate. If relevant, make sure you also have access to your national security number - just in case!

BAT AWAY THOSE PESKY EXCUSES

This month my biggest excuse, worry or fear about my trip has been:

I can combat this excuse/worry/fear with the following actions:

MONTH 5
BE GRATEFUL, THINK POSITIVELY

'To live is the rarest thing in the world. Most people just exist.'

- OSCAR WILDE

Now that you have a clear plan for your travels, it's time to take stock of everything you have around you. The next few months are your time to reflect on what you have at home, and to prepare yourself for the enormous adventure you're about to embark on. This month is all about developing your sense of mindfulness and setting yourself up for as much financial freedom as possible when you travel.

SIMPLIFY YOUR SURROUNDINGS

Traveling is all about letting go of the home comforts that hold you back. Embrace new experiences with humility, simplicity and kindness. Look around your home and assess where you may be overindulging, and where you might be overspending in your current lifestyle. Write down five things you can live without.

1. _____

2. _____

3. _____

4. _____

5. _____

PLAN YOUR BUDGET WITH TRAVEL IN MIND

The number one excuse, worry or fear most people have about traveling is how they will pay for it. This is a personal challenge and needs to be looked at with reference to your unique circumstances. The trick is to determine how long you will need to sustain yourself for without earning any new money, then to create a rough outline of how much money you will need each month based on the average living costs for your chosen destinations. This gives you a savings target.

Once you've done this, saving enough money for your trip is a simple, 3-step process that can be adapted to most circumstances:

Step 1: Assess your current financial situation. See where you can trim back on some of the luxuries you may be able to do without. For example, you might be stopping for a coffee in the station every day as part of your commute, or keeping a few active subscriptions to online streaming services you seldom use.

Step 2: Re-evaluate your financial priorities with travel in mind. Create a system that allocates your surplice expenditure to travel. Instead of buying a coffee on the way to work, transfer the cost of the coffee into your dedicated travel account. You may want to match this amount as a personal contribution to transfer into your savings.

Step 3: Increase your income. You might find a side hustle, sell a few items of furniture, sell your home to fund your adventures or work hard for a promotion.

CREATE AN EXPENDITURE RE-ALLOCATION ACTION PLAN

Work out which things you can do without and how much they cost. Next, multiply this amount by the number of times you purchase the item in a month. Finally, multiply the monthly cost by the number of months you have available to save, and you'll quickly see how easy it is to save a substantial amount of money for your travels by making a few small sacrifices every day.

THINGS I CAN LIVE WITHOUT	COST PER DAY OR ITEM	COST PER MONTH	MONTHS TO TRAVEL DATE	TOTAL TO SAVE
Daily Coffee	$4.60	$138	8 Months	$1104

TOP TIP - Always pay yourself first. That way you won't spend the money on something else before you manage to save it!

MONTH 5: TRACK YOUR WEEKLY PROGRESS

WEEK 1

WEEK 2

WEEK 3

WEEK 4

'Live life with no excuses, travel with no regret.'

- OSCAR WILDE

NOTES:

'Whether you think you can, or you think you can't - you're right.'

- Henry Ford

SPEND TIME WITH THE RIGHT PEOPLE

Once your savings plan is in place and you no longer need to worry about how you're going to get your finances in order, evaluate who you are spending the most time with, and how they're impacting your life. Life is too short to worry about other people's negative opinions.

Use this time to develop your sense of self, and your ability to fill your life with positive, mindful energy. It's important to spend as much as time as possible with the people you love the most before your departure date, as you might not get to speak to them as often as you would like to while you're away.

GET RID OF NEGATIVE EXCUSES

My top excuse this month is: _____

I've overcome this excuse by: _____

MONTH 5 CHECKLIST:

☐ ASSESS PERSONAL FINANCES & CREATE AN STRONG ACTION PLAN

☐ REASSIGN SURPLACE SPENDING TO A DEDICATED TRAVEL FUND

☐ ACTIVELY DISTANCE FROM PEOPLE WHO BRING NEGATIVE ENERGY

☐ MAKE THE TIME TO VISIT IMPORTANT PEOPLE AS OFTEN AS POSSIBLE

MONTH 6
LOVE IT ... OR CHANGE IT!

'Your travel life is in your own hands, and your hands only!'

- TRAVELPEEGEE

By this stage you should have the bones of your travels plans well in place. Your flights are booked, your visa applications are in progress, and you've created a solid plan for saving enough money to really enjoy yourself. It's now time to flesh it all out with detailed plans and juicy ideas.

SET UP YOUR SOCIAL MEDIA ACCOUNTS

While you're away, you'll want to keep up with people from home to share your experiences with others. Many people write books during or after their travels, so take the time to set up a good blog and dedicated social media presence, if this is something you're interested in.

You may also like to set up a personal website to keep your followers up to date, which can be expanded on at any time to include affiliate links as a way of making money at any time in the future.

If you're unsure about having a blog or website, set it up anyway. Traveling opens unbounded opportunities for personal growth, so you might come back to it later.

BUILD AN INSPIRING NETWORK

One of the best ways to start your travel research is using social media apps like Instagram and YouTube. Try to follow influential globetrotters and digital nomads who are working their way through the countries you intend to visit.

The secret is to follow as many people as possible to learn from their ideas.

You might find you had an idea in your head, such as visiting the beaches in India, then watched a few videos online and changed your mind. If this happens, change your idea into something that completely blows you away. Your flight route is there to guide you, but the rest of your itinerary is an open book for you to fill with your wildest dreams!

TOP TIP

Find a way to record your adventures and try to do this every day while you're away. Write down little stories and keep lists of the places you've been - the longer you travel, the harder it becomes to remember everything.

Some people keep a small journal, others use blog websites like WordPress. Even if you don't publish anything, working in draft form keeps your best memories easily accessible.

EXPAND YOUR TRAVEL INSPIRATION COLLECTION

Immerse yourself into the world of travel. Fill your boots with books and movies to whet your appetite for all things travel related. If you're going to New Zealand, binge on *Lord of the Rings* and watch *Hunt for the Wilderpeople.* If you're heading to Bali or India watch *Eat, Pray, Love* and read *The Jungle Book*.

Actively seek out those things that inspire your soul every day. Try new restaurants and sample the foreign cuisines, take a Vietnamese cooking class to develop your taste for the flavors, or read up on the history of Costa Rica and the Rio Carnival.

Inspiration breathes further inspiration into newer, fresher ideas. The more you look at things that keep you motivated, the richer your travel experiences will be.

MONTH 6 CHECKLIST:

- ☐ SET UP A DEDICATED TRAVEL ACCOUNT ON INSTAGRAM
- ☐ OPEN A WORDPRESS ACCOUNT TO START A BLOG
- ☐ FOLLOW ONLINE INFLUENCERS WITHIN THE WORLD OF TRAVEL
- ☐ KEEP AN ADRESS BOOK FILLED WITH USEFUL CONTACTS
- ☐ DECIDE HOW YOU WILL DOCUMENT YOUR EXPERIENCES
- ☐ BUILD UP A COLLECTION OF TRAVEL RELATED BOOKS & MOVIES
- ☐ SAMPLE THE FOREIGN CUISINE OR ATTEND A RELEVENT CLASS
- ☐ GET TRULY EXCITED ABOUT EVERY PART OF THE TRAVEL EXPERIENCE

MONTH 6: TRACK YOUR WEEKLY PROGRESS

WEEK 1

WEEK 2

WEEK 3

WEEK 4

'Live life with no excuses, travel with no regret.'

- Oscar Wilde

NOTES:

'Whether you think you can, or you think you can't - you're right.'

- HENRY FORD

MONTH 7
TAKE YOUR ADVICE FROM THE RIGHT PEOPLE

'The first condition of understanding a foreign country is to smell it.'

- RUDYARD KIPLING

Traveling the world is a playground for learning. It takes you back to the basics of childhood where every lesson comes from solving problems and figuring out how things work. While most lessons are enjoyable, there will also be times when you're pushed outside of your comfort zone with limited resources. These scenarios are a huge part of why people like to travel but can require you to think on your feet!

BRUSH UP YOUR SAFETY SKILLS

There are a few essential skills you can learn before you leave that will help you stay safe in every situation, especially if your travel is infused with outdoor adventures!

Every person should know the basics of how to survive in an emergency, and how to create simple hacks that can make life more comfortable. You don't need to know how to suture wounds with a fishing hook, but it's worth knowing what to do if you get bitten by something unfamiliar, or if you injure an ankle on a hiking trip.

Take a basic first aid course, either online or in your local area, and start gathering some essential items for your emergency survival kit. Bandages, Steri-strips, alcohol wipes, antihistamine tablets, insect repellent and painkillers are a great start.

RESEARCH THE WEATHER

Make sure you have a clear understanding of what to expect so you can start finding the right kinds of clothing for the environments you're going to visit. If you'll be spending winter months at a ski resort, you'll need an excellent waterproof coat. If you'll be going on safari in Africa, adaptable waterproof clothing and light cotton layers will serve you well. Try to cross-purpose as many clothes as possible.

COUNTRY TO VISIT	TIME OF YEAR	AVERAGE CLIMATE	ESSENTIAL CLOTHING	PURCHASED

TOP TIP - Aim for layered clothing that can be adapted to many different climates. Some specialist clothing items can be bought or rented abroad, such as skiing or diving gear. Op shops and flea markets can also be a great way to pick up cheap essentials.

MONTH 7: TRACK YOUR WEEKLY PROGRESS

WEEK 1

WEEK 2

WEEK 3

WEEK 4

'Live life with no excuses, travel with no regret.'

- Oscar Wilde

NOTES:

'Whether you think you can, or you think you can't - you're right.'

- Henry Ford

TOP TIP

Join a mountain club or outdoor group in your local area. Mountain clubs often have free courses to help you upskill for the great outdoors!

Ask for details in your local camping store.

OVERCOME YOUR EXCUSES BY STAYING INFORMED

This month my biggest excuse, worry or fear about survival has been:

I can combat these excuses with the following actions:

MONTH 7 CHECKLIST:

☐ TAKE A BASIC SURVIVAL & FIRST AID COURSE

☐ RESEARCH THE WEATHER FOR ALL DESTINATIONS

☐ START AQUIRING THE RIGHT KINDS OF LAYERED CLOTHING

☐ WATCH SOME YOUTUBE VIDEOS ABOUT SURVIVAL HACKS

MONTH 8
MAKE EXPONENTIAL USE OF YOUR TIME

'Time flies. It's up to you to be the navigator.'

- ROBERT ORBEN

Now that you know how to stay safe abroad, it's essential you protect yourself financially with robust travel insurance - shop around as much as possible! When getting your travel insurance, make sure you're covered for all the key things below:

- ✈ **Length and scope of your policy:** make sure your policy covers you for the full duration of your trip, and for all the countries you plan to visit. You might need a special backpacker policy for longer journeys.

- ✈ **Cancellation**: this covers you if you, or someone you need to take care of, becomes too ill for you to travel before you leave your home country.

- ✈ **Curtailment:** this is in case your trip needs to get cut short due to illness, someone at home becoming ill, or an international emergency.

- ✈ **Medical cover**: this covers you for local treatment if you become sick or injured while you're away.

- ✈ **Dangerous activities:** make sure you're covered for extreme outdoor sports, including skiing, horseback riding, hiking and diving.

MONTH 8: TRACK YOUR WEEKLY PROGRESS

WEEK 1

WEEK 2

WEEK 3

WEEK 4

'Live life with no excuses, travel with no regret.'

- Oscar Wilde

NOTES:

'Whether you think you can, or you think you can't - you're right.'

- Henry Ford

AVOID POTENTIAL PITFALLS WITH ADEQUATE PROTECTION

> ### TOP TIP
>
> Purchase your travel insurance policy as soon as possible to cover you for cancellation if something unexpected comes up before you're due to travel. Make sure you declare any pre-existing medical conditions to your insurance provider when you buy your policy.

LET GO OF YOUR EXCUSES

This month my top travel excuse has been:

I can stop making this excuse by:

MONTH 8 CHECKLIST:

- ☐ RESEARCH TRAVEL INSURANCE
- ☐ CHECK THE KEY POINTS ARE SUFFICIENTLY COVERED
- ☐ PURCHASE A TRAVEL INSURANCE POLICY
- ☐ DECLARE PRE-EXISTING MEDICAL CONDITIONS FOR INSURANCE

MONTH 9
PROTECT YOURSELF TO STAY HEALTHY

One of the most important things to do when preparing for travel is to get the right vaccinations to protect yourself against diseases that may not be prevalent in your home country. Only a GP or travel clinic can advise you on the vaccinations you need, however, some countries do require proof of a yellow fever vaccination.

Make a list of the countries you're visiting and plan your vaccinations in advance. You'll usually need to make an appointment, and not all shots can be given at the same time, so timing it well is as important as getting the vaccinations.

TOP TIP

A valuable resource for researching travel vaccines is the U.S. State Department website, where you will also find useful information about any travel advisories that may be in place for your itinerary.

Keep a list of any areas of concern that you may wish to keep an eye on later.

Some of the most important vaccinations to consider are for malaria, cholera and yellow fever. Always talk to your GP about your suitability for these inoculations.

ORDER REPEAT PRESCRIPTIONS

You'll be away for some time, so it's important to resolve any underlying health concerns before you travel. Take some time to compile a list of questions about your health that you may like to ask your GP about.

If you have any prescription medication, or regularly take medication containing any controlled substances such as codeine or morphine, it's essential you carry the written prescription with you on any flights you take. Some countries are extremely strict about medication, so always pack this in your checked-in luggage if possible.

Countries to Visit	Jabs Needed	Date of Vaccination	Months Covered

Some vaccinations cover you for a couple of years, others for a lifetime!

PUT ASIDE YOUR EXCUSES BY PLANNING WISELY

This month my biggest worry, concern or excuse has been:

I can stop making this excuse by:

MONTH 9 CHECKLIST:

- ☐ RESEARCH RECOMMENDED VACCINATIONS
- ☐ PLAN A VACCINATION SCHEDULE & MAKE APPOINTMENTS
- ☐ ORDER REPEAT PRESCRIPTIONS
- ☐ DISCUSS UNDERLYING HEALTH CONCERNS WITH THE GP

MONTH 9: TRACK YOUR WEEKLY PROGRESS

WEEK 1

WEEK 2

WEEK 3

WEEK 4

'Live life with no excuses, travel with no regret.'

- OSCAR WILDE

NOTES:

'Whether you think you can, or you think you can't - you're right.'

- HENRY FORD

MONTH 10
SHOW UP, NO MATTER WHAT!

'Still round the corner there may wait a new road or a secret gate; and though I oft have passed them by, a day will come at last when I shall take the hidden paths that run west of the moon, east of the sun.'

- J.R.R. TOLKIEN

It's nearly time to set off on your magical adventure! You've worked hard, saved some money, organized your documents and prepared yourself for taking hold of every opportunity that presents itself.

QUIT YOUR JOB, WITH NO EXCUSES

Yep, you heard right! Now that you're on your way it's time to write up your letter of resignation and let your employer know you'll be traveling soon. Depending on your circumstances, you may want to negotiate coming back to work in the future, or simply head off and never look back. Quitting a job is incredibly liberating! Be nice, be open and be honest... you'll reap the rewards every step of the way!

When you travel, your life has the capacity to change exponentially as you live, learn and grow through your experiences. Many people come back to find they no longer fit into the life they held before they left home. The simple rule of thumb is if you're not bound to something, lighten your load and let it go...

PUT YOUR HOUSE ON THE MARKET, IF SELLING, OR RENT IT OUT

If you're a homeowner and plan to travel for a few years, or hope to turn travel into a full-time lifestyle, you may be able to use your home as a source of future income. Talk to your bank or local financial advisor to establish the best way to make your property work for you while traveling. If you are considering selling your property it may be more lucrative to rent it out and earn a monthly rental income.

FREE YOURSELF FROM MAKING EXCUSES

This month I've been making excuses because:

I can stop making excuses by thinking differently:

MONTH 10 CHECKLIST:

- ☐ CHOOSE A CLEAR FINAL WORKDAY TO SUIT YOUR ITINERARY
- ☐ RESIGN IN WRITING, WITH CLEAR EXPECTATIONS
- ☐ LEAVE ON A POSITIVE NOTE, WITH DOORS OPEN
- ☐ ASK FOR WRITTEN REFERENCES TO TAKE WITH YOU
- ☐ UPDATE YOUR LINKEDIN PROFILE & ASK FOR TESTIMONIALS

MONTH 10: TRACK YOUR WEEKLY PROGRESS

WEEK 1

WEEK 2

WEEK 3

WEEK 4

'Live life with no excuses, travel with no regret.'

- Oscar Wilde

NOTES:

'Whether you think you can, or you think you can't - you're right.'

- HENRY FORD

MONTH 11
TAP INTO YOUR TRAVEL CREATIVITY

'The important thing is not to stop questioning. Curiosity has its own reason for existing.'
- ALBERT EINSTEIN

Your departure date is getting closer and closer, so it's time to rustle up your excitement and get your gear together. Keep your load as light as possible!

OFFLOAD ANY UNNECESSARY EXPENSES

Think about some of the accounts you may no longer need, including things like insurance policies, mobile phone accounts and utility bills. Contact your suppliers and make sure you're clear on how to close your accounts correctly. You don't want to end up with any surprise bills while you're away.

If you do need to keep some accounts open, set up direct debits and make sure these will always have funds available to pay them. You might not always have access to the internet while traveling, so it's really important to make sure your accounts can take care of themselves.

RENT OUT YOUR APARTMENT OR GIVE NOTICE TO MOVE OUT

Be clear with your landlord about when you will leave, or if you will sublet, and make sure you repaint the walls and redecorate as appropriate to get your deposit back.

INVEST IN A FEW WISE PIECES OF QUALITY GEAR

All the best backpacker's lodges in the world have nooks and crannies filled with various items left by those passing through - books, kitchen mugs, blankets, hoops, sports gear and hammocks are regularly passed on to new arrivals or those who have stayed so long they just blend in with the staff.

Travelers require extraordinarily little to get by. Invest in a few essential items, and buy things as you need them. Use this handy list below as a guide to help you decide what to purchase for your travels.

- ✈ Quality sleeping bag, suitable for at least 3 weather seasons
- ✈ Sturdy backpack, with soft sides that can be compressed on all sides
- ✈ First aid kit, packed into a waterproof carry bag
- ✈ Universal plug adapter, and a spare USB cable
- ✈ A pen, and a small notebook
- ✈ Comfortable socks, the kind that don't slip down in your shoes

TOP TIP

Visit your local camping store to purchase a few compression sacks. These are useful for arranging your belongings in your backpack and help remove any space-consuming air so you can fit more in it.

MONTH 11: TRACK YOUR WEEKLY PROGRESS

WEEK 1

WEEK 2

WEEK 3

WEEK 4

'Live life with no excuses, travel with no regret.'

- OSCAR WILDE

NOTES:

'Whether you think you can, or you think you can't - you're right.'

- HENRY FORD

IF YOU'RE UNSURE, LEAVE IT BEHIND

As you're getting your gear together, run everything through a mental checklist, asking yourself: Is this heavy? Do I need this? Will I miss this? If you answer yes to any of these questions, leave it at home. You'll always be able to buy what you need locally, so pack light and carry less.

BECOME TOO EXCITED TO MAKE EXCUSES

This month I've been concerned about:

Which I have solved by:

MONTH 11 CHECKLIST:

- ☐ CLOSE ACCOUNTS THAT WON'T BE NEEDED WHILE YOU'RE AWAY
- ☐ GIVE THE LANDLORD NOTICE TO MOVE OUT, OR SUBLET
- ☐ PURCHASE A QUALITY SLEEPING BAG & SOFT-SIDED BACKPACK
- ☐ GET A UNIVERSAL PLUG ADAPTER, AND A SPARE USB CABLE
- ☐ BUY COMPRESSION SACKS, AND NEW SOCKS

MONTH 12
TAKE DECISIVE TRAVEL ACTION

'A ship in harbor is safe, but that's not why ships were built.'

- JOHN A. SHEDD

The air is filled with excitement and you will be too, soon! Everything is in place, your excuses are long gone and you're about to embark on the adventure of a lifetime. Take a moment to breathe it all in and enjoy every second!

TIDY YOUR LIFE ADMIN

Go through all your accounts, bills and paperwork to double check that everything is taken care of. Close accounts, redirect your mail, check your direct debits are in place and notify your bank that you'll be traveling.

Check the exchange rates and fees for using your credit and debit cards overseas to work out which will be the cheapest to use abroad. You may also like to change some money into the local currency for emergencies.

Contact your insurance providers to see if you need to change your policy if you're away from home, and cancel any extras that aren't needed. You might be able to save some money by being smart with your bills.

MONTH 12: TRACK YOUR WEEKLY PROGRESS

WEEK 1

WEEK 2

WEEK 3

WEEK 4

'Live life with no excuses, travel with no regret.'

- OSCAR WILDE

NOTES:

'Whether you think you can, or you think you can't - you're right.'

- Henry Ford

VISIT IMPORTANT PEOPLE

You may be busy this month, but make sure you spend some quality time with your friends and family. Before you go, make sure they have the details of your social media accounts, as well as your known contact details, so they can follow your journey from home.

MONTH 12 FINAL CHECKLIST:

- ☐ MAKE SURE ALL ACCOUNTS ARE CLOSED
- ☐ OFFLOAD ANY EXPENSES THAT ARE'NT NEEDED WHILE AWAY
- ☐ GET YOUR DEPOSIT BACK FOR YOUR APARTMENT
- ☐ SET UP DIRECT DEBITS FOR OPEN ACCOUNTS
- ☐ PACK AS LIGHTLY AS POSSIBLE, USING COMPRESSION SACKS
- ☐ PACK UNDERWEAR
- ☐ DON'T PACK TOO MANY TOILETRIES
- ☐ PRINT OFF ALL FIGHT & VISA DOCUMENTS
- ☐ MAKE SURE YOU HAVE YOUR PASSPORT
- ☐ MAKE SURE YOU HAVE YOUR COPIES OF IDENTITY DOCUMENTS
- ☐ MAKE SURE YOU HAVE YOUR INTERNATIONAL DRIVER'S LICENSE
- ☐ PLACE MEDICAL PRESCRIPTION DOCUMENTS INTO HAND LUGGAGE
- ☐ PACK NON-ESSENTIAL MEDICATION INTO CHECKED LUGGAGE
- ☐ DECIDE WHICH CREDIT CARDS TO USE WHILE TRAVELING
- ☐ SPEND QUALITY TIME WITH FRIENDS & FAMILY

Travel is a deeply personal experience that will change your life, regardless of who you are or where you have come from. To travel is to open yourself up to the new, to embrace others as they present themselves to you, and to find yourself in places you never could have imagined.

Enjoy every minute, and take the challenges along with every amazing opportunity that comes your way. Regret nothing, say yes to everything, and have an absolute blast!

SHARE YOUR EXPERIENCES

Now that you're an expert at creating a life of travel, I encourage you to share your experiences. Please leave a review to inspire others to start their own adventures!

See you out there!

TravelPeeGee

Made in United States
North Haven, CT
31 December 2021

13920726R00037